STUNT PERFORMERS ON FILM

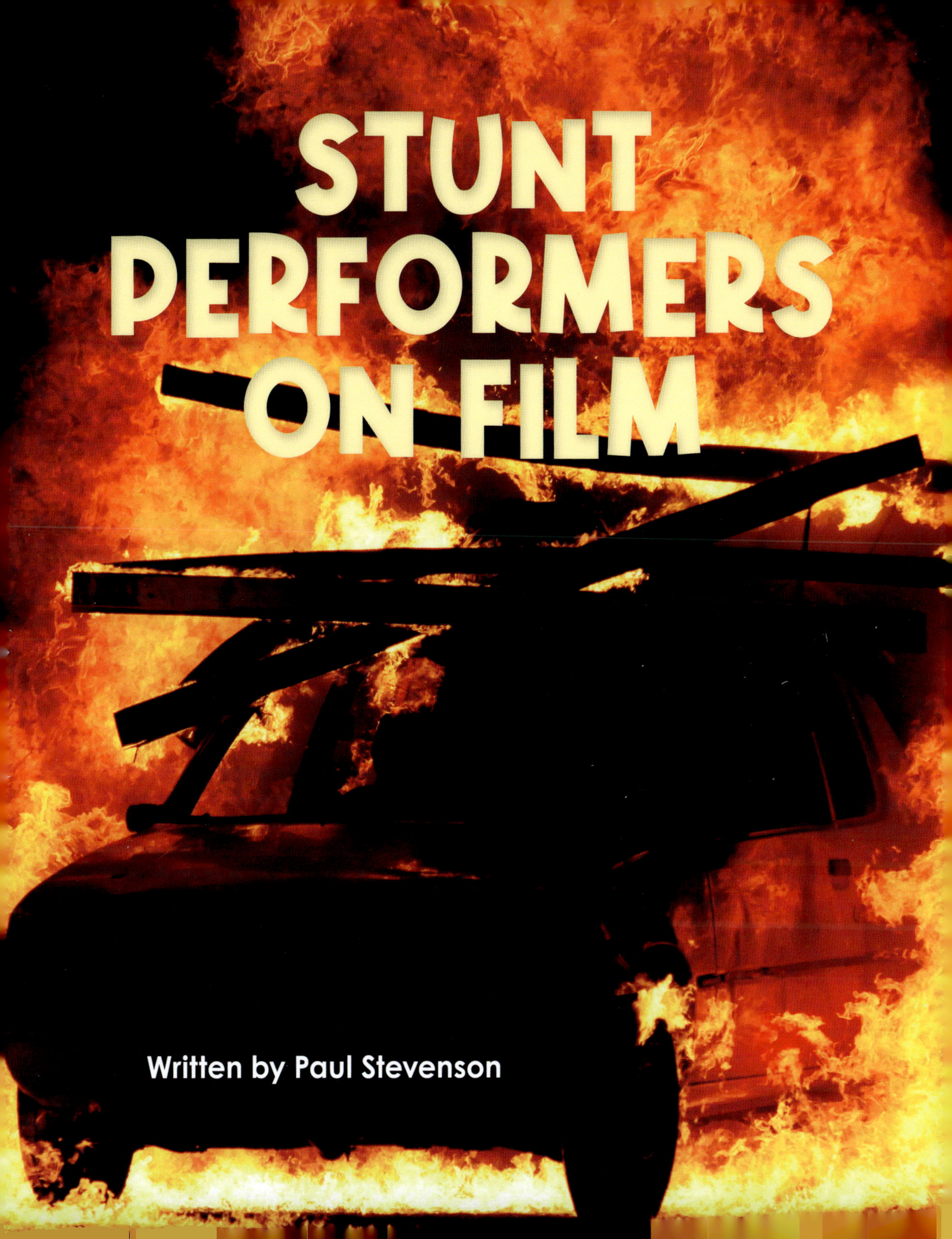

Written by Paul Stevenson

CONTENTS

First published in 2024 by
Hungry Tomato Ltd
F15, Old Bakery Studios,
Blewetts Wharf, Malpas Road,
Truro, Cornwall,
TR1 1QH, UK.

Thanks to our editor, Julie Tofflemire.

A CIP catalog record for this book is available from the British Library.

ISBN 9781835690154
Manufactured in the USA

Discover more at
www.hungrytomato.com

Neither the publisher nor the author shall be liable for any bodily harm or damage to property whatsoever that may be caused as a result of conducting any of the activites in this book.

DISCLAIMER:

The stunts featured in this book have been done by experienced stunt performers. Do not attempt to copy any of these stunts.

All words in **BOLD** can be found in the glossary.

ACTION!

Action movies are exciting to watch! An action hero leaps from a burning building. A car flies through the air and smashes into a truck!

It looks as if the actors do these stunts. However, most stunts are done by stunt performers.

When a stunt is too difficult or too dangerous for the actors to do, stunt performers take the place of actors.

Stunt performer Greg Brazzell drives a car into a truck.

Water bottles get thrown out of the car's way!

EARLY DAYS

Stunts have come a long way since the early days of film.

1900s TO 1930s

At first, Hollywood actors performed their own stunts, but audiences wanted more excitement. So, film **directors** started using stunt performers so they could include more daring stunts.

Rodeo rider Rose Wenger, also known as Helen Gibson, **doubled** for Helen Holmes in a Western movie serial.

1940s TO 1950s

Performers developed ways to make stunts as safe as possible. They used trampolines, cardboard boxes and straw to break high falls.

1960s TO 1970s

New **technology** was developed to make stunts look more real. **Air rams** and air bags were invented.

Air rams throw a performer into the air.

Air bags give stunt performers a soft landing.

REACHING NEW HEIGHTS

As action films became more popular, new and more exciting stunts were created. Stunt performers could even "fly" through the air!

1980s TO 1990s

Action films, such as *Rambo*, *Indiana Jones* and *Die Hard*, became very popular. They were packed with stunts and **special effects**.

Many films used stunts with wire work. The performers fly through the air on wires.

Stunt vests are attached to wires for stunts performed in the air.

2000s AND BEYOND

Many film directors now use computers to make realistic action scenes. But real stunts are still popular!

The Matrix movies used wire work and martial arts, along with other visual effects.

The actors were filmed against a green screen. Then a background was added using a computer. The wires were removed by computer too. The actors look as if they are flying above the ground.

THE THREAT OF CGI

As computer-generated imagery (CGI) improves, filmmakers will be able to create even more over-the-top scenes that look realistic.

What does this mean for stunt performers?

Motion capture technology is used for recording the movements of a performer to create a digital character.

With CGI, any stunt is possible. Some stunt performers worry that their jobs will be taken over by computers.

A performer wears a motion-capture suit to record a scene.

Thanos, from the Marvel Cinematic Universe, was created by CGI.

However, many people think that stunts will be less exciting if they are just computer-generated. When an actual person is performing a stunt, the scene feels more real.

So, the best solution may be a combination of CGI and human performers. That means mind-blowing stunts can still have that human touch.

PIONEERING PERFORMERS

Actors as far back as the silent film era pioneered the art of stunts. There were no computers, so the only way to show a stunt was to do it!

BUSTER KEATON (1895 TO 1966)

Buster Keaton was a silent film actor. He did many of his own stunts. In this famous scene, a house falls on Keaton. The house misses him because he is standing below an open window.

YAKIMA CANUTT (1895 TO 1986)

Canutt did his first film stunt in 1915. He got his last film **credit** in 1975! Canutt and his friend the actor John Wayne developed fighting and stunt **techniques**.

Yakima Canutt

PEARL WHITE (1889 TO 1938)

Pearl White was an actor who did many of her own stunts. She starred in *The Perils of Pauline*.

Her most famous stunt was when she was tied to railroad tracks in front of a speeding train!

STUNT LEGENDS

Being a legend in the stunt world takes skill, strength and fearlessness. It means pushing yourself to the limit.

DAR ROBINSON (1947 TO 1986)

In 1980, Dar Robinson jumped off the CN Tower in Toronto, Canada. He did this stunt for the movie *High Point*. His hidden parachute opened just 300 feet (90 m) from the ground!

Robinson liked to set stunt records. He was the first person to skydive out of a plane at 12,000 feet (3,600 m) while riding in a small sports car.

Robinson does tricks on a trampoline hanging from a helicopter.

JACKIE CHAN (BORN IN 1954)

Jackie Chan started his career as a stunt performer in **Bruce Lee** Kung Fu movies. Chan's movies mix **slapstick** comedy with Kung Fu action.

One spectacular stunt included a three-story drop through two **awnings**. In another, he fell into a bed of red-hot coals!

Even in his 70s, Jackie Chan is still doing his own stunts!

STUNT-PERFORMING STARS

Some stars don't like to sit on the sidelines. They do many of their own stunts.

DANIEL CRAIG

As James Bond, Daniel Craig performed many of his own stunts. These included a stair fall and an underwater rescue scene. Craig got bruises and cuts and even had his front two teeth knocked out!

Craig leaps from a rooftop in *Quantum of Solace.*

SCARLETT JOHANSSON

When Johansson first took on the role of Black Widow for *Iron Man 2*, she had never filmed a fight scene before.

She trained hard and mastered the **choreography** for the fights. She also learned how to do wire work.

TOM CRUISE

Cruise is known for doing jaw-dropping stunts:

- Climbing the tallest building in the world (*Mission: Impossible - Ghost Protocol*)
- Hanging onto the side of a plane (*Mission: Impossible - Rogue Nation*)
- Driving a motorcycle off a cliff (*Mission: Impossible - Dead Reckoning Part 1*)

PLANNING A STUNT

The goal of a good stunt is for it to look real, but also be safe. Stunt coordinators do a lot of planning for action scenes.

STEPS FOR PLANNING A STUNT

1. Read the **script** and make notes on the action scenes
2. Discuss how the stunt should look with the film director
3. Work out how much the stunt will cost
4. Do a "recce", visiting the film **location**
5. Choose the stunt performers

Preparations for a scene

"When I'm planning a stunt, safety is everything. I have to think what if..."
- **Steve Truglia, stunt performer and stunt coordinator**

The stunt performers practice the stunt.

In a stunt fight, the performer's hand never makes contact with the face. Skilled stunt performers and clever **camera angles** make a stunt fight look real.

VEHICLE STUNTS

Stunt performers drive at high speeds. They help to create exciting chase scenes in films.

The performers develop their driving techniques at a stunt driving school. They learn how to skid, spin and even drive on two wheels!

Scenes are planned and set up carefully before a shoot.

Stunt drivers can practice on an **enclosed** track. They need to make sure they can perform the high-risk moves safely and accurately.

Even chariots need stunt drivers! In the 1959 movie *Ben-Hur*, the stunt driver had a nearly **fatal** stunt. He lost his balance during a planned bump. Fortunately, he stayed in the chariot.

The chariot race in Ben-Hur

BURN SCENES

Many movies have scenes where people are on fire! These are called burn scenes. They are very dangerous to perform.

The stunt performers wear fireproof clothes. They use a special gel to stop their skin and hair burning.

The performers must not breathe when they are on fire. They could burn their lungs or breathe in **poisonous fumes**.

The burn is carefully timed. In case of an emergency, medical professionals are standing by. The stunt crew is ready to put out the fire.

Stunt performer Steve Truglia performs a fire burn.

STUNTS IN THE AIR

Stunts don't just have to remain on the ground. Performers have been finding creative ways to do amazing stunts in the air too.

HIGH FALL STUNTS

High fall stunts are very dangerous. Every second of the fall is planned, practiced and tested.

Stunt performers learn how to fall and how to land. If a stunt performer lands in the wrong position, they can be badly hurt.

Giant air bags give stunt performers a safe place to land.

SKYDIVING STUNTS

For the best shots of skydiving stunts, the camera must be in the air too! The cameraperson wears a camera attached to their helmet.

JUMPING BETWEEN BUILDINGS

Experienced stunt performers can jump between buildings without wires.

In 1990, stunt performer Roy T. Anderson set a record with his 28-foot (8.5-m) jump between two buildings in Toronto, Canada. The stunt took seven months to plan!

TRICKS OF THE TRADE

Stunts need to look real, but that doesn't mean they need to be real. Filmmakers can make things look more dangerous than they really are.

Film sets have windows and items such as bottles made from special materials. These materials smash easily and safely. They are known as "breakaway effects".

The "glass" can be made from rubber or even sugar!

THE EDGES OF BREAKAWAY GLASS AREN'T SHARP LIKE NORMAL GLASS.

For dramatic scenes, stunt performers can use special furniture that is made to break easily. This is especially important when it's broken over someone's head!

The weapons you see in films, like axes and knives, are usually made of rubber or plastic. They look real from far away, but they won't cause serious damage or injury to the actors.

STUNT DOUBLES

Stunt coordinators need to find the right person for the right stunt.

When choosing a stunt performer, stunt coordinators look for two important things. The stunt performer should:

1. be trained and **insured** to do the stunt.
2. be a good "double" for the actor.

Monique Ganderton has been a stunt performer for over 20 years. She performed as well as coordinated stunts for *Avengers: Endgame*. She was also a stunt double for Charlize Theron in *Atomic Blonde*.

Stunt double
Monique Ganderton

Actress Charlize Theron

Tanoai Reed has performed stunts in many Hollywood films. He is the stunt double for Dwayne "The Rock" Johnson.

It's not surprising that these two have a similar look – they're cousins!

Stunt double Tanoai Reed

Actor Dwayne "The Rock" Johnson

Even if filmmakers can't get a perfect match, they can use makeup and wigs to make the double and actor more alike. They also use far-away shots or different angles to hide the stunt double's face.

AND REMEMBER, IN ACTION SCENES, THE CHARACTER IS USUALLY MOVING FAST!

GETTING INTO STUNT WORK

Here are some tips for getting into stunt work.

- You will need good physical fitness. Stunt performers take part in sports that are good for general fitness, such as running and swimming.

- Stunt performers need useful skills such as **martial arts**, rock climbing, skydiving or riding motorbikes or horses.

- Try getting work as a film extra (for example, a person in a crowd scene). This helps you to get a license to work in films and on TV. It's also a good way to find out about film sets and to meet stunt coordinators.

Extras getting ready for a historical scene

GLOSSARY

air ram – a piece of equipment that throws a performer into the air.

awning – a piece of cloth that stretches out over a door or window to block the rain or sun.

Bruce Lee – a martial arts (see right) expert who made martial arts popular in movies.

camera angles – the positions from which the camera shoots the film.

choreography – the planned steps and movements in a dance or a fight scene.

computer-generated imagery (CGI) – realistic-looking images that have been created using a computer.

credit – a film credit is when a person's name is shown at the end of a film.

director – the person who chooses the actors and tells them what to do in each scene of a movie, play or TV show.

doubled – (to double) when someone takes an actor's place in a movie.

enclosed – with walls or fencing all around.

fatal – causing death.

fumes – substances such as gas or smoke that have a strong smell or that are dangerous when breathed in.

insured – having paid money into a fund in case something bad happens to you. If something bad does happen, the fund pays money to help you.

location – the place where a movie or TV show is filmed.

martial arts – ways of fighting without weapons, such as Kung Fu, karate and judo.

pioneered – (to pioneer) to be the first person to do something.

poisonous – causing illness or death when taken into the body.

rodeo – a contest in which cowboys show off their horse-riding skills.

script – the words the actors say in a movie, play or TV show.

slapstick – comedy based on people being clumsy on purpose – for example, falling over or bumping into things.

special effects – tricks that filmmakers use to make the audience think that something is real in a movie.

technique – a way of doing something.

technology – using scientific knowledge in useful ways, such as making machines or systems better.

INDEX

Picture credits:
(t=top; b=bottom; m=middle; l=left; r=right):
Bettmann/Corbis: 13br.Big Pictures: 16b. Corbis Sygma: 9b. Everett Collection/Rex Features: 9t, 13t, 21b. Getty Images: 6br. RGA: 10mr. Rick Doyle/Corbis: 4bl, 4br, 5bg. Scot Leva, Precisionstunts.com: 7tr. Shutterstock: 2-3bg, 22b; Alex from the rock 25br; Denis Markarenko 28br; Dmitry Eagle Orlov 20b; Doug McLean 7b; Evgeniyqw 27b; Flystock 30br; Gorgev 19bg; GorodenKoff 10bl; Jaguar PS 28bl; Jonathan Weiss 12b; Kathy Huchins 29mr; Lars Christensen 1bg; Lev radin 17tr; Metamorworks 11bg; Mikhail Romanov 8b; Motorsports Photographer 17bl; Mr.B-King 21t; New Africa 26ml; Patinthanon Pongsuansri 10br; Pavel L Photo and Video 24b; Photostock360 18ml; Sabath 27t; She 14-15bg; Showcake 26mr; Sky Antonio 25t, 31b; Tinseltown 15ml, 29ml; Zhukovvvlad 30m. Wikimedia commons: 6ml.